MW01602508

Singing as We Journey

CHRISTOPHER EDERESINGHE

Copyright © 2002
Christopher Ederesinghe

Library of Congress Control Number: 2002095245
ISBN: 0-9726096-0-1

Cover/book design: rachel Ortiz
Typeset: Sabon 12/14

Printed in the United States by Morris Publishing
3212, East Highway 30
Kearney, NE 68847
1-800-650-7888

CONTENTS

Foreword

This book should be owned by every pastor. To know the scriptural setting or the story behind a hymn makes that hymn spring to life.

Author, pastor, teacher, Chris Ederesinghe has given us a treasure-trove of information that can be used by choristers, teachers and pastors to help us understand the depth and width of each musical presentation from the viewpoint of the hymn's author. Members will sing with understanding and a greater appreciation.

Doug Kilcher
Ministerial Director

Mid-America Union Conference
of Seventh-day Adventists

Liconln, Nebraska
February 2002

Acknowledgments

The inspiration for this book can be traced back to my parents, who fostered my musical interests since I was just five years old when I began taking piano lessons. Years later while preparing for the ministry, some of my teachers at Spicer Memorial College continued to encourage me to delve into the background and history of hymns. Still more recently, in 1984, while serving as a missionary in South America, I was invited to conduct a Week of Prayer at a small church on the outskirts of Santiago, Chile. The Lord helped me to build a series of messages based on hymns and hymn stories. These now form the basis for Part Two of this book. After returning to the United States from that missionary assignment, I resumed my studies at Andrews University, in Berrien Springs, Michigan. With the encouragement I received from my professors, including Dr. C. Warren Becker, the late Dr. Kenneth Strand, and the late Dr. C. Mervyn Maxwell, I continued to focus my studies toward finding ways of making hymn-singing more meaningful to Christians. The workshop on congregational singing, which I developed under the influence of my teachers and the guidance of the Lord, features a congregational hymn festival which includes the hymns I have described in Part One of this book.

My thanks are also due to Mrs. Rachel Ortiz, who volunteered her time and her skills to do the page-proofing of the manuscript in preparing it for publication.

THE AUTHOR

Preface

This book is intended to encourage every traveler on life's pilgrimage to keep on "singing as we journey," thus making their own journey, as well as that of their fellow pilgrims, a time of joyful worship in song. The stories behind these hymns, their authors and composers make their singing more meaningful.

It is the author's desire that the contents of this book will add to the spirit and the understanding of hymn singing, especially as these hymns are included in both private and public worship.

Introduction

The children of Israel began their wilderness wanderings with a song of victory, the song of Miriam. On various other occasions throughout their forty years of travel, they united their voices in joyful praise to God. The record of their journey to the earthly Canaan carries a wealth of symbols for Christians who are on their spiritual pilgrimage toward the heavenly Canaan.

> "Often on the journey was this song repeated cheering the hearts and kindling the faith of the pilgrim travelers. Thus their thoughts were uplifted from the trials and difficulties of the way, the restless, turbulent spirit was soothed and calmed, the principles of truth were implanted in the memory, and faith was strengthened."[1]

Any journey involves preparation, departure, and anticipation of reaching the destination, anxiety and longing, and a joyous reunion at journey's end. Hymns expressing the Christian's pilgrim journey reflect these same sentiments.

Indeed, many a hymn reminds us that we are "strangers and pilgrims on the earth" (Hebrews 1:13).

Consider the following example:

> "We are travelling to our home,
> Blessed home, blessed home,
> We are travelling to our home,
> Singing as we journey."

"Toward a city out of sight,
Where will fall no shade of night,
For our Savior is its Light,
Singing as we journey."[2]

Each of the following chapters features one or more hymns which highlight the above aspects of Christian pilgrimage.

Every one of these pilgrim hymns described in this book has its own story. In many cases, each hymn reflects some aspect of its author's or composer's own spiritual pilgrimage.

The apostle Paul urges the Christian pilgrim to use singing as a means of mutual encouragement and edification:

> "Speaking to yourselves in psalms, and hymns and spiritual songs, singing and making melody in your heart to the Lord." — Ephesians 5:19.

> "Teaching and admonishing one another in psalms and hymns and spiritual songs." — Colossians 3:17

Such use of singing obviously extends beyond the limits of the formal worship service. Mutually encouraging one another, and communicating elements of truth must be a part of Christian living; thus, "singing as we journey" will truly become a part of the Christian's earthly pilgrimage.

The Israelites sang as they journeyed through the wilderness, on their way to the earthly Canaan. The Christian pilgrim, too, will express his joyful praises to God, while travelling to the heavenly Canaan.

Part One:
Singing About the Journey

CHAPTER I

Preparation for the Journey

Choosing the Best Guide
Guide Me O Thou Great Jehovah
Seventh-day Adventist Hymnal No. 538

he children of Israel faced the challenge of the unknown as they stepped out toward the Red Sea. Along with their leader Moses, all they had to guide them were the "fire and cloudy pillar." Farther along, they received manna, "bread of heaven," and water which flowed out of the "crystal fountain." However, from the very beginning, the Exodus experience involved an abandoning of their own plans and submitting to God's plans for their lives.

William Williams, a youthful medical student attended an open-air meeting conducted by Welsh evangelist, Howell Harris. Like the Israelites of old, Williams, too, experienced the call to abandon his personal plans and goals in favor of God's plan for his life. He accepted God's call to become an evangelist. Through the rest of his life, his evangelistic ministry took him more than three thousand miles on foot and horseback, preaching the gospel throughout his native Wales. Of more than eight hundred hymns which he wrote during his lifetime, this is his best known.[3] It has been translated into English and many other languages.

Every Christian needs to acknowledge the need to trust in God's power to lead him through this spiritual pilgrimage.

Like the author of this hymn, the sincere believer can testify:

"I am weak, but Thou art mighty,
Hold me with Thy powerful hand"

When chased by Pharaoh and the Egyptian army, the Israelites had no hopes of survival; the Red Sea ahead offered them no consolation either. Only as they obeyed the Lord's seemingly impossible instructions to march into the water were they delivered from danger.

The Christian, travelling as a "pilgrim through this barren land," must depend only on Christ Who said "I am the Bread of Life" for spiritual sustenance; He alone can:

"Feed me till I want no more."

The Christian pilgrim will also find rest and refreshment in Jesus while on his weary pilgrimage:

"Open now the crystal fountain,
Whence the healing stream doth flow"

As he travels on through life's wearisome pilgrimage, the Christian is assailed by many fears and doubts; These include doubts regarding the future, doubts regarding eternity, and many other kinds of uncertainties. The hymn writer prays with confidence, in the third stanza:

"When I tread the verge of Jordan,
Bid my anxious fears subside;
Bear me through the swelling current,
Land me safe on Canaan's side"[4]

On this hazardous journey through unknown territory, and fraught with spiritual and physical dangers, the safest Guide is Jesus. One day soon, when the journey is over, every believer who makes this choice will find his experience reflected in the final lines of this hymn:

"Songs of praises' songs of praises,
I will ever give to Thee."

The most important aspect of the Christian's preparation for this spiritual pilgrimage is a total commitment to God's guidance.

Recognizing Our Pilgrim Condition
I'm a Pilgrim
Seventh-day Adventist Hymnal No. 444

The Christian who has accepted Jesus as His Guide for his pilgrimage must also be willing to accept his own status as a pilgrim and sojourner on this earth. Two hymns in the *Seventh-day Adventist Hymnal* portray the transient nature of the Christian's earthly life. The first of these, "I'm a Pilgrim" comes from the pen of an early follower of William Miller, Mary Stanley Bunce, the daughter of a Congregational minister, who later married Charles B. Dana. This hymn expresses the longing of many an early Millerite Adventist, the longing to move on toward his heavenly goal:

> I'm a pilgrim, and I'm a stranger;
> I can tarry, I can tarry but a night

Whereas the *Seventh-day Adventist Hymnal* contains the three stanzas which emphasize the early Adventists' longing for "the city to which I journey...," the *Church Hymnal* contains three other stanzas, where the hymn writer-pilgrim bids farewell to her neighbors, mother, sister, brother, and "drear earth by sin so blighted"[5]

The children of Israel had to leave the dubious security of Egyptian bondage when they set out on their journey to the Promised Land; they had to leave behind the onions, leeks, and garlic, (Numbers 11:5) and the fleshpots (Exodus 16:3) of Egypt, for the less luxurious prospect of a long and tedious trek through the desert, in quest of an unknown des-

9

tination. Christians in many lands today face similar uncertainties as they step out in faith to begin their journey towards the heavenly Canaan. Often, wealth, social status, parental and family approval are denied to those who desire to join this "happy band of pilgrims." Yet, only those who recognize the transient nature of all these temporal luxuries in contrast to the eternal riches in glory will make that decision to move on with God's people. The Christian, who recognizes the transient nature of this earthly existence, is one who has made a firm decision to make that spiritual journey. The sights and sounds of this world can easily tempt one to abandon his long-cherished plans to reach the journey's end. The committed pilgrim pleads with those who would have him defer or delay his onward march,

"Do not detain me, for I am going
To where the fountains are ever flowing ..."

This hymn expresses the Christian pilgrim's readiness to leave neighbors, relatives, and earthly possessions, in order to continue journeying to the promised land. The true Christian pilgrim is concerned for the salvation of others; at the same time, he warns them against letting hesitation become an excuse for the pilgrim to delay or cancel his journey. The refrain repeats the same sense of urgency: "I can tarry, I can tarry, but a night."

I'm but a stranger here.
(Seventh-day Adventist Hymnal No. 445)

Thomas Taylor, the author of the second of these "pilgrim" hymns, a retired Congregational minister, wrote this hymn, just before his own own earthly pilgrimage ended. Like Abraham, who sojourned in the land of promise as in a strange country, dwelling in tabernacles... and "looked for a city which had foundations, whose Builder and Maker is

10

God" (Heb 11:9, 10), the Christian pilgrim can honestly join Taylor as he sings:

"Short is my pilgrimage, heaven is my home."
Heaven is my fatherland, Heaven is my home."

Does the way we live, act, think, and speak, lead others to recognize us as citizens of that heavenly fatherland? Many religions require or urge their believers to make long and tiresome pilgrimages to man-made shrines or places difficult to reach. Followers of Islam hope to gain merit by making at least one pilgrimage to Mecca during their lifetime. Hindus from all parts of India make the journey to the Ganges, to bathe in the waters of that river which they hold sacred. Buddhists from various Asiatic countries make the hazardous ascent up Sri Pada, to the shrine of the Buddha's footprint, in Sri Lanka, during the annual pilgrim season in the month of May. (Westerners have named this mountain Adam's Peak based on a legend that Adam set foot there on his way out of Eden.) Many Christians visit the holy land where Jesus walked while here on earth. However, all of these travelers, regardless of their religious persuasion, return from their periodic pilgrimages to their everyday life. The Christian's spiritual pilgrimage, on the other hand, is a one-way journey. There is no turning back. While it leads to the heavenly kingdom, the journey itself does not result in merit gained by the believer. Rather, it consists of the Christian's response to God's call: "Come out from among them and be ye separate." (2 Corinthians 6:17)

Thus, the Christian pilgrim needs to make a conscious decision to "follow the Master." This involves a separation from a worldly life-style. This, in turn will help instill an intense longing for the joys of the eternal homeland, while helping the believer recognize that he is indeed a sojourner in this world, and that he is a citizen of the heavenly country.

Rejection by the world will not matter, when one is confident that the Lord has accepted him as a citizen of the heavenly country, through the merits of Jesus. Only through the strength supplied by Christ is such a decision possible. Only in His strength can the Christian pilgrim have the confidence to face the right direction, as he sets out on this spiritual journey. The hymns discussed in the next chapter reflect that firm determination which the pilgrim must exercise.

CHAPTER 2

Determination and Dedication

Facing the Right Direction
He Who Would Valiant Be
The New Advent Hymnal No. 530.

obody has illustrated the Christian's pilgrimage to the celestial city so beautifully and graphically as John Bunyan, in his classic *Pilgrim's Progress*. Few are aware that this tinker of Bedford, who spent much of his life in prison for his faith, has also written this hymn. The *New Advent Hymnal,* the hymnbook used by Seventh-day Adventists in Britain, contains this hymn that expresses so emphatically the Christian's resolve to be a pilgrim:

> "He Who would valiant be,
> 'Gainst all disaster
> Let Him in constancy,
> Follow the Master
> There's no discouragement
> Shall make him once relent
> His first avowed intent
> To be a pilgrim"

> "Whoso beset him round
> With dismal stories
> Do but themselves confound
> His strength the more is
> No foes shall stay his might,

Though he with giants fight
He will make good his right
To be a pilgrim"

"Since, Lord, Thou dost defend,
Us with Thy Spirit
We know we at the end
Shall life inherit.
Then fancies flee away!
I'll fear not what men say,
I'll labor night and day
To be a pilgrim."

Like Christian, the leading character in Bunyan's *Pilgrim's Progress*, the twenty-first century Christian pilgrim also needs to let nothing deter his "first avowed intent to be a pilgrim." There will be many who would "beset him... with dismal stories," but, as the hymn says, "His strength the more is."

"The powerful effect of Bunyan's sermons resulted in severe persecution and, for the crime of preaching, he was imprisoned for more than twelve years. Much of his time in jail was devoted to the writing of books, one of which was Pilgrim's Progress. He never intentionally wrote any hymns, but his 'He who would valiant be' from the second part of Pilgrim's Progress, 1684, was added to hymnic compilations by nineteenth century editors."[6]

This hymn, like the rest of Bunyan's book, expresses the importance of facing the right direction throughout our pilgrim journey. Like the prophet Isaiah, every Christian must "set (his) face like a flint" (Isaiah 50:7) in all spiritual matters.

Accepting the Risks of the Journey
Oft in Danger, Oft in Woe
The New Advent Hymnal, No. 501

The words of this hymn were found written on the back of one of Kirke White's mathematics papers at Cambridge University, where White was a student. The first stanza was altered to the form in which it is now published, while the second, third, and fourth stanzas were written by Mrs. Fuller-Maitland when the latter was still a girl of fourteen.[7]

This hymn is a reminder of the dangers and woes that the Christian pilgrim is sure to meet along the way. The very first stanza points out that this pilgrimage involves a battle against evil; the Christian needs to:

"Fight the fight, maintain the strife
Strengthened with the Bread of Life"

The second stanza continues to use the battle metaphor, and urges the Christian soldier to "March in heav'nly armour clad," while the third stanza keeps up the tone and theme of encouragement for the battle-weary soldier-pilgrim:

"Let not sorrow dim your eye
Soon shall every tear be dry;
Let not fears your course impede,
Great your strength if great your need."

In the final stanza, this hymn points the Christian soldier to the promised victory in Christ:

"Onward then to glory move,
More than conquerors ye shall prove:
Though opposed by many a foe
Christian soldiers, onward go."

Brightening the Journey With Song
Marching to Zion
(The New Advent Hymnal, No. 454;
Seventh-day Adventist Hymnal No. 422)

The poetic propensities evident in Isaac Watts (1674-1748) from a very young age often aggravated his parents and teachers. However, in later life, he wrote many hymns, several of which are still sung by Christians today. This hymn is a good example of Watts's work.

The refrain lends a lilting rhythm to the pilgrims' onward march towards the heavenly Caanan. The second stanza throws out a challenge to "those... who never knew our God," thus making it imperative that:

> "Children of the heavenly King
> May speak their joys abroad"

An unconfirmed story is told of the choir at a New England church. It is rumored that, due to some trivial misunderstanding, the choir members decided to "go on strike," and, hence, were seen seated in the rear of the church, rather than in the choir stalls, for several weeks in succession. One Sunday morning, so the story goes, the minister decided to use "Marching to Zion" as the opening hymn for the service. By the time the congregation reached the middle of the second stanza,[8] the "strike" was over.

> "Let those refuse to sing,
> Who never knew their Lord,
> But children of the heavenly King,
> May speak their joys abroad,
> May speak their joys abroad."

While these words were being sung, the choir members rose, and returned, one by one, to their assigned places in the choir stall, and the "strike" was called off. Certainly, this incident emphasizes the fact that God's pilgrim people cannot ever afford to "go on strike" as did that choir; Indeed, as Watts points out in his hymn, only "those who never knew our God" may refuse to sing.

Like the children of Israel who spent many dreary years wandering through the wilderness, the Christian pilgrim, too, passes through many a wearying and boring experience, not to mention numerous trials, while on his heavenward journey. However, if he truly loves the Lord, the very thought of what awaits him at the journey's end will inspire him to sing as he continues on his spiritual pilgrimage:

> "Then let our songs abound,
> And every tear be dry,
> We're marching through Immannuel's ground,
> To fairer worlds on high."

Not just an occasional song or two at Sabbath School and church each week, but, "let our songs abound!" Only the Zion-bound pilgrim can truly experience that kind of joy, which overflows in sacred song. Like Paul and Silas who sang through that eventful night in the jail at Phillippi, the Christian pilgrim, too, needs to burst out in songs of praise to the Redeemer. Singing through the darkest nights of one's experience can help maintain one's focus on his heavenly goal. The converse is also true, as expressed in this hymn. Anticipation of the "hills of Zion" which "yield a thousand sacred sweets" can elicit hymns of gratitude, despite the afflictions that assail the Christian *en route* to "Immanuel's land." Having thus made a firm determination to follow the best available Guide on this one-way journey, the Christian needs, next, to start moving on in the direction of that heavenly city, the New Jerusalem. The hymns considered in the next chapter deal with God's promises to sustain the faithful heaven-bound pilgrim as he makes his journey in the direction of his heavenly home.

CHAPTER 3

Heaven Bound Pilgrims

Setting Our Course Right
O Happy Band of Pilgrims
Seventh-day Adventist Hymnal No. 629.,
The New Advent Hymnal, No. 539

hen the children of Israel left Egyptian bondage to set out on their pilgrim journey to the promised land, there was singing and rejoicing among that "happy band of pilgrims." Centuries later, Joseph of Sicily, (b. 800 A.D.) wrote the original Greek version of this hymn. He had become a slave in Crete, resulting from his capture by pirates. Later on, after he was set free, this ex-slave became a monk in Constantinople. No doubt, this hymn expressed his feelings as he joined the happy band of Christian pilgrims on their way to the heavenly Caanan. Because of his prolific output of hymns, this ninth century poet was later known as "Joseph the Hymnographer." John Mason Neale, a British linguist, translated this hymn from its original Greek into English.[9]

The author of this hymn urges Christian pilgrims to move onward in their pilgrimage,

> "With Jesus as your Fellow,
> With Jesus as your Head,"

He further reminds the believer that Jesus, Who once carried the cross "as your due," now wears the crown also "for you."

Joseph the Hymnographer encourages the "happy band of

pilgrims" to labor and hunger as Jesus did, and to consider this earthly pilgrimage as being "such a light affliction" in comparison with "so great a prize" as awaits the pilgrim at the end of his journey.

Indeed, this hymn provides the rationale for the Christian's spiritual pilgrimage: the cross and the crown.

Total Dependence on God
Throughout our Pilgrimage
Through All The Changing Scenes of Life
The New Advent Hymnal, No. 245

This "new version" of the thirty-fourth psalm first appeared in Nahum Tate and Nicholas Brady's *A New Version of the Psalms of David Fitted to the Tunes Used in Churches*, which was published in 1696. This version of Psalm 34 has survived over three centuries.[10] Like its original scriptural version, this paraphrase of Psalm 34 expresses the true believer's confidence and trust in God "through all the changing scenes of life, In trouble and in joy,"

> "The praises of my God shall still
> My heart and tongue employ,"

In the context of the Christian's spiritual pilgrimage, this hymn expresses the psalmist's (and hence, the Christian's) confidence in God protective power under all circumstances. It is also an invitation to "all that are distressed" to take comfort "from mine example," and "to make but trial of His love," because:

> "Protection He affords to all,
> Who make His name their trust"

Certainly, as the Christian continues on his spiritual pilgrimage, the "changing scenes of life" can swing back and forth many times between "trouble" and "joy." At the "trouble" end of the spectrum, the temptation is to refrain from praising God. However, the authors of this hymn have aptly paraphrased the psalmist's words in Psalm 34:1, "I will bless the Lord at all times: His praise shall continually be in my mouth."

Along their tedious and danger-fraught wilderness journey, the Israelites needed to depend totally on the protection that God alone could provide. As the third stanza of this hymn emphasizes,

> "The hosts of God encamp around
> The dwellings of the just"

The Christian pilgrim can do no better than to trust in the protective power of God, as he travels on in his spiritual pilgrimage toward the heavenly Canaan. While on this journey, they will then "have nothing else to fear," since "your wants shall be His care."

Steadfastness: A Basic Requirement
Through The Night of Doubt and Sorrow
(The New Advent Hymnal, No. 541)

This hymn, originally titled "Unity and Progress," was written in Danish. It was first published in Copenhagen in 1859. Bernhardt Severin Ingemann was a prolific poet of national reputation. Ingemann's father was a clergyman, and wanted his son to follow in his steps. Sabine Baring-Gould's English translation of this hymn was published in various hymnals in 1867 and 1875.[11]

Note the lively marching rhythm of the tune, which well illustrates the onward march of the Christian pilgrims,

> "Singing songs of expectation,
> Marching to the promised land."

From start to finish, this hymn continually reminds Christian pilgrims of their ultimate goal. They face a "night of doubt and sorrow," as they continue "Marching to the promised land" (stanza 1).

The final stanza brings that ultimate goal back into focus, as the Christian is reminded that,

> "Soon shall come the great awakening,
> Soon the rending of the tomb:
> Then the scattering of all shadows,
> And the end of toil and gloom." (stanza 5)

However, before that "great awakening" of the dead in Christ takes place, the Christian pilgrim must keep marching onward in Christian unity with his fellow-believers:

> "Brother clasps the hand of brother,
> Stepping fearless through the night" (stanza 2)

Such Christian unity does not take place unless it is based on the One in Whom we are united:

> "One the light of God's own presence,
> O'er His ransomed people shed,
> Chasing far the gloom and terror,
> Brightening all the path we tread." (stanza 3)

Have we made Jesus our Guide for this pilgrim journey? Have we made that total commitment? Do we depend entirely on Him for our spiritual and physical sustenance? Will we be ready to greet Him at our journey's end?

As the following chapter deals with the end of the Christian's pilgrimage, the reader would do well to review this musical pilgrimage thus far, while retaining a forward look towards the heavenly Canaan, the eventual goal of the Christian's earthly pilgrimage. Thus, the Christian pilgrim must not only seek divine guidance to set his course right. He must become totally dependent on God, and resolve to move onward with steadfast resolution under His guidance, while remaining unwaveringly loyal to Him. Only such a close relationship with Christ can enable us to keep on "singing as we journey," and, even after that journey has ended, to keep on singing throughout the ages of eternity.

CHAPTER 4

Nearing Journey's End

Faith in the Unseen and Unknown
There's a Land That is Fairer Than Day
(Seventh-day Adventist Hymnal No. 428)

s the Christian pilgrim approaches his journey's end, his faith is tested more and more intensely than during the earlier stages of the journey. Persecutions, trials, physical and spiritual handicaps, all of these trying experiences become increasingly severe. As defined in the Book of Hebrews, faith is "the substance of things hoped for, the evidence of things not seen." (Heb 11:1). In this context, the entire eleventh chapter of Hebrews presents what might well be called the Bible's "Faith Gallery." All of those in this "Hall of Faith" looked forward, like Abraham, to "a city which had foundations, whose builder and maker is God." (Heb 11:10). The writer sums up his description of these faithful pilgrims, in verse 13 of the same chapter:

> "These all died in faith, not having received the promises,
> but having seen them afar off, and were persuaded of
> them and embraced them, and confessed that they were
> strangers and pilgrims on the earth."

Such is the faith and hope expressed in this song which points the pilgrim to the end of his journey, "the land that is fairer than day," which "by faith we can see ... afar," where the Father prepares us a dwelling place. Every true Christian pilgrim expresses that same steadfast faith in the hereafter. And, if, in that hereafter, we plan to

"sing on that beautiful shore,
the melodious songs of the blest,"

we certainly need to get some practice while still here below!

Sanford F. Bennett, the author of "The Sweet By and By," wrote this well-known gospel song, in response to his friend's expression. Joseph P. Webster, a music teacher, apparently entered Bennett's place of business in a melancholy mood, one day in 1868. Upon Bennett's inquiry as to the reason for his gloom, Webster is said to have replied, "It will be all right by and by." Bennett immediately began writing the words. When he handed the paper to Webster, the latter played the melody on his violin, and jotted down the notes. Within the next thirty minutes, the song was born.[12] Webster's residence is preserved today as a museum in Elkhorn, Wisconsin.[12]

This song aptly expresses the Christian pilgrim's vision of the "land that is fairer than day," which he sees afar "by faith," and, where he hopes to "sing on that beautiful shore, the melodious songs of the blest." It also expresses the gratitude of the believer:

"To our bountiful Father above,
We will offer a tribute of praise,
For the glorious gift of His love,
And the blessings that hallow our days."

Courage for the Tired Pilgrim
Long Upon The Mountains Weary
Seventh-day Adventist Hymnal No. 447

This hymn "presents the early Advent believers as God's precious flock that has passed through "grievous trials." "The narrative depicts the flock as following 'the light of truth,' feeding on God's word, heeding His precepts. The final stanza comprises several images of Adventist theology: 'clouds descending,' 'saints entombed arise,' and 'The redeemed in anthems blending Shout the victory through the skies.'[13]

Annie Rebekah Smith, the author of this hymn, longed for "that golden city fair." She expressed the longing of every Christian pilgrim,

> "O, we long for Thine appearing;
> Come, O Savior, quickly come!
> Blessed hope our spirits cheering,
> Take Thy ransomed children home."

As the weary pilgrims travel on in anticipation of their journey's end, their longing for that triumphant end to all of their weariness intensifies with every new bend in the road. They have "compassed this mountain (Mount Seir), long enough," (forty years in the case of Israel on their way to the earthly Canaan!) and are awaiting the command, "Turn you northward." (Deut. 2:3).

Exhortations to Remain Faithful Unto the End
O Brother, be Faithful
Seventh-day Adventist Hymnal, No. 602

Uriah Smith, Advent pioneer, author of *The Prophecies of Daniel and the Revelation*, (Washington, D.C: Review & Herald Publishing Association, 1944,) wrote the words of this hymn. It was first published in the September 27, 1853 issue of the *Review and Herald*.

At a time when hymnals were not readily available to those congregations who were often widely scattered, many hymns were written to fit secular tunes that were familiar to the believers.

The Review issue containing this hymn also instructed the readers to sing it to the tune of a song familiar at that time, "Be Kind to the Loved Ones at Home."[14]

This is a song of encouragement to the pilgrim believers. In the context in which it was written, it repeatedly exhorted each pilgrim "brother" to remain faithful, for, "soon Jesus will come" (stanza 1), and because "He soon will descend... soon shalt thou hear thy Saviour pronounce the glad word,

"Well done, faithful servant, thy title is clear,
To enter the joy of thy Lord." (stanza 3)

The remaining stanzas bring reassurance to the Christian pilgrim:

"...the city of gold,
Prepared for the good and the best
Is waiting, its portals of pearl to unfold,
And welcome thee into thy rest." (stanza 2)

In the final stanza, the travel-weary pilgrim is given good reason to rejoice as he nears his journey's end:

"O brother, be faithful! eternity's years,
Shall tell for thy faithfulness now,
When bright smiles of gladness shall scatter thy tears,
A coronet gleam on thy brow."

Heir of the Kingdom
Seventh-day Adventist Hymnal, No 594.

The anonymous author of this hymn challenges the weary pilgrim to remain alert and awake while approaching "so near thy blest home." (stanza 1.) The words of this stirring hymn point the believer to various signs of our Lord's soon return:

"Earth's mighty nations in strife and commotion,
How canst thou tarry in sight of the prize?" (stanza 2)

In the third stanza, the hymnwriter pleads with the heaven-bound pilgrim to resist worldly temptations:

"Stay not, O stay not for earth's vain allurements!
See how its glory is passing away;
Break the strong fetters the foe hath bound o'er thee
Heir of the kingdom, turn, turn thee away."

As the "heir of the kingdom" approaches the close of his journey, he is reminded to:

"Watch for the glory of earth's coming King:
Lo! o'er the mountain-tops light is now breaking:
Heirs of the kingdom, rejoice ye and sing." (stanza 4)

Joyful Anticipation
How Sweet Are The Tidings That Greet The Pilgrim's Ear
Seventh-day Adventist Hymnal No. 442

This anonymous early Advent hymn brings joyful tidings to the weary pilgrim "as he wanders in exile from Home." The weary pilgrims (who) will to glory go" are made glad upon being reassured that:

"Soon, soon will the Savior in glory appear,
And soon will the kingdom come."

This reassuring message brings the comforting news that
their journey will soon be over, and that they will be reunit-
ed shortly with their fellow-pilgrims who have fallen asleep
along the way, when:

"The mossy old graves where the pilgrims sleep
Shall be open as wide as before,
And the millions that sleep in the mighty deep
Shall live on this earth once more."

Just Over the Mountains, in the Promised Land
Church Hymnal, No. 642

Charles P. Whitford of Vermont was the son of Millerite parents who became First-day Adventists. Charles joined the
Seventh-day Adventist Church in 1867, after having worked
at the Battle Creek Health Reform Institute.[15] In this hymn,
he pictures the Christian pilgrim nearing journey's end. Even
as Moses viewed the promised land from the heights of
Mount Pisgah, Whitford pictures the weary Christian who:

" ... can view our homeland of eternal rest." (stanza 1)

This hymn reminds the weary pilgrim of the scriptural
prophecies concerning the eternal homeland, while pointing
him forward, as:

"...with raptured vision we can see it there,
with its walls of jasper and its mansions fair." (stanza 2)

In the third stanza, Whitford reminds the pilgrim of the
scriptural qualifications of "those who enter that city," those
who "keep God's commandments, faith of Jesus, too," as
described in Revelation 14:12.

In the final stanza, the invitation is extended,

My brother, my sister, will you meet us there,
In that land of sunshine where there'll be no care?
Accept of God's message, and to Him be true,
Then when Jesus cometh He will call for you.

The reassuring words of the chorus ring out after each stanza:

"We are nearing home, We are nearing home,
See the splendor gleaming from the domes afar!
See the glory streaming through the 'gates ajar!"
There we soon will enter, never more to roam,
Hear the angels singing! We are nearing home!
We are nearing home."

After their long and tedious pilgrimage through the desert, their first glimpses of Caanan must certainly have brought them a sense of relief. Moses saw it, but was not allowed to enter. (Deuteronomy 34:1-5).

In faith, the Christian pilgrim views something far superior to all that Moses saw that day. The hymns discussed in the conclusion to Part One give the Christian pilgrim a sense of anticipation for the heavenly Caanan.

Heaven: The Goal of Every Christian Pilgrim

he three final hymns presented in this section of the book are descriptive of heaven, the Christian's ultimate goal, in the context of the Christian's spiritual pilgrimage.

When All My Labors and Trials Are O'er
Seventh-day Adventist Hymnal No. 435

This hymn points to the Christian's blessed hope, the hope of meeting Jesus face to face. Many hymns have been written on this theme. However, this hymn lays special emphasis on the Christian's anticipated joy,

> "Just to be near and to look on His face,
> Will through the ages be glory for me."

Charles Gabriel, learned to play on the reed organ at his parents' farm home in Wilton, Iowa. Although many of his earliest compositions were secular in nature, he developed a strong interest in hymn-singing at an early age. His parents often invited their neighbors over to join them in hymn-singing at their home, after all of their farm chores were done. Charles Gabriel's inspiration for the "Glory Song" came from the superintendent of the Sunshine Rescue Mission in St. Louis, Missouri, Ed Card, who had earned the nickname "Old Glory Face," because he punctuated his sermons with the exclamation, "Glory!"[16]

In each of its three stanzas, Gabriel presents the joy of being in the presence of Jesus, in contrast with one aspect of the Christian's anticipated glory and joy in the hereafter.

In the first stanza, being finally "safe on that beautiful shore" pales into insignificance, in comparison to being in the presence of Jesus:

> "Just to be near the dear Lord I adore
> Will through the ages be glory for me."

In stanza 2, seeing Jesus face to face "will through the ages be glory for me,"

> "When by the gift of His infinite grace,
> I am accorded in heaven a place.
> The final stanza describes the glad reunion, when,
> Friends will be there I have loved long ago,
> Joy like a river around me will flow,"

However, the hymn writer maintains his emphasis on the supreme joy and glory he anticipates when he sees his Saviour face to face, with the closing words of that stanza,

> "Yet, just a smile from my Saviour, I know,
> Will through the ages be glory for me."

The refrain highlights the recurring theme that is already so clear in all three stanzas,

> "When by His grace I shall look on His face,
> That will be glory, be glory for me."

A Song of Heaven and Homeland
Seventh-day Adventist Hymnal No. 472.

Ira D. Sankey, well-known gospel singer and musician of the late 1800's and early 1900s, recalls how this hymn was found in a collection of 20 hymns sent him by Eben Rexford, landscape gardening editor of the *Ladies' Home Journal*:

> "In the year 1901, Mr. Eben Rexford... wrote to me, asking a donation of 50 copies of Gospel Hymns for a poor church, saying he would give me 20 new hymns in exchange. I sent the books and received the hymns, among which I found 'A Song of Heaven and Homeland', which I soon set to music, and which I consider to be one of my best compositions."[17]

The "new song" which Jesus puts in the heart of the believer is an echo of the "new song" in which all who are faithful will someday participate when they enter heaven.

In Sankey's well-known hymn collection, *Sacred Songs and Solos*,[18] a line from Revelation 14:3, "And they sung as it were a new song before the throne," was printed above the music of this hymn.

Are we listening for that song, the "song of heaven and homeland"? Then do not grow weary in your pilgrim journey.

Invitation to Join in Pilgrimage
Will You Go?
Church Hymnal, No. 368

Unlike the worldling who, upon discovering some source of material wealth, selfishly keeps that knowledge to himself, the Christian pilgrim extends the invitation to all who wish, to join him on his heavenward journey. A hymn of anonymous authorship, No. 368 in the *Church Hymnal*, aptly expresses such an invitation:

"We're bound for the land
Of the pure and the holy,
The home of the happy,
The kingdom of love."

Nearly half of this hymn describes the joys of "that blessed land" where "neither sorrow nor anguish" is found. In the final stanza, the earnest appeal is made,

"And yet, guilty sinner,
We would not forsake thee,
We halt yet a moment as onward we move;
O, come to thy Lord!
In His arms He will take thee,
And bear thee along to the Eden above."

The invitation comes to every person for whom Jesus died, every individual who should join that happy band of heaven-bound pilgrims:

"Will you go, will you go,
Will you go, will you go,
O say, will you go to the Eden above?"

Part Two:
Songs of Experience
Along the Pilgrim Journey

CHAPTER 5

How Shall We Sing The Lord's Song in a Stange Land?

The Strange Land: Then and Now

The Strange Land: Why Were They There?

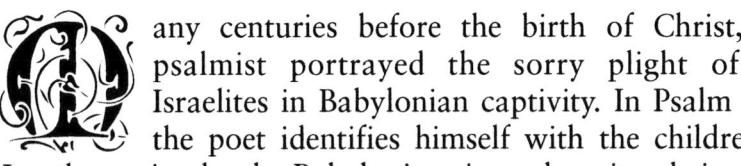 any centuries before the birth of Christ, the psalmist portrayed the sorry plight of the Israelites in Babylonian captivity. In Psalm 137, the poet identifies himself with the children of Israel weeping by the Babylonian rivers, hanging their musical instruments on the willow trees, because they were unable to sing the "songs of Zion" "in a strange land." (Psalm 137:3,4) In the first two verses of the same psalm, the poet records the people's lamentation: "By the rivers of Babylon, there we sat down, yea, we wept when we remembered Zion." (Psalm 137:3,4) Their lamentations were greeted by the mocking taunts of their captors who demanded that they sing "the songs of Zion." (verse 3)

Some years later, the prophet Isaiah reminded the captive Israelites of the reason for their captivity. "O that thou hadst hearkened to my commandments, then had thy peace been as a river, and thy righteousness as the waves of the sea (Isaiah 48:18). However, the prophet continues with a reassuring command: "Go ye forth of Babylon, flee ye from the Chaldeans, *with a voice of singing* declare ye, tell this, utter it even to the end of the earth, say ye, The Lord hath redeemed His servant, Jacob. (Isaiah 48:20)

While the Babylonian captivity was an historical reality, it also has a symbolic significance to the Christian. John the Revelator records his prophetic vision of the severe persecution that Christians were to face. The prophecies of the Book of Revelation point to spiritual "Babylon" which derives its power and authority from the "dragon" which is Satan (Revelation 13:2). In this and other related passages, John identifies this spiritual Babylon as the power responsible for that persecution. In a sense, all humanity has been taken hostage by the dragon who represents Satan in the Book of Revelation. Jesus has paid the ransom price. Victory is available to all those who accept His ransom plan. That plan is only available through the shed blood of Jesus, the Lamb of God (Revelation 13:12).

The Israelites' Longing to Return to Jerusalem

In the text quoted at the beginning of this chapter, the psalmist describes the sad lamentation of the Israelites, as they remembered their beloved city of Zion. The writer of the Book of Revelation points the Christian to the heavenly city, the New Jerusalem (Revelation 21:1, 2) The Book of Revelation also points to certain events and situations, some of which have already taken place, while others are yet in the future. However, the underlying theme beneath all of these prophetic, utterances, as well as the entire book, seems to be an emphasis on the worship of the true God. Revelation begins with John's first reaction to his vision of Jesus, the Alpha and Omega (the first and the last letters of the Greek alphabet, symbolizing the "beginning and the end.") (Revelation 1:11-18.) It closes with the ultimate experience of God's people worshiping in the very presence of God, as foretold in Revelation 21:22. In fact, chapters 14 and 18 of the book sound forth a clear call to God's people. These chapters summon God's people to "come out" of Babylon (Revelation 18:4), and separate themselves from spiritual

Babylon and the false worship that it represents. The three angels featured in Revelation 14 declare the fall of spiritual Babylon, while calling people to worship the Creator, and to identify themselves with His true worshippers. In doing so, they will prepare for that grand heavenly worship celebration, where they will sing a "new song" of praise to the One who has redeemed them from destruction. (Revelation 5;11).

Nowhere else in this final book of the Bible is the worship theme better summarized than in the messages of the three angels portrayed in Revelation 14:6-12. The first of these heavenly messengers warns of the judgment hour which "is come." That same angel also proclaims aloud the call to "worship God" as the Creator of this universe. (verses 6,7). This clearly points to God's true day of worship, the only Biblically endorsed day to be celebrated in honor of God's creative power—the seventh-day Sabbath, as referred to in Exodus 20:8-11.The second angel announces the defeat of spiritual Babylon (verse 8), and is echoed in Revelation 18:4, with the call to "come out" (of Babylon) "that ye be not partakers of her sins, and that ye receive not of her plagues. Following close behind these first two messengers, the third angel identifies God's true believers, the "saints," who "keep the commandments of God, and the faith of Jesus," while, at the same time, pronouncing the fate of the captors, and of those who refuse to accept God's salvation (verses 9-12).

The captive Israelites took up the lamentation only "when we remembered Zion." Likewise, the Christian who finds himself surrounded by the "strange land" that this old world represents, needs to have a sense of "homesickness" for heaven. Certainly, this sin-ravaged world offers no inspiration for anyone to sing "the songs of Zion." This can only take place when one accepts the conditions of citizenship in the heavenly kingdom. (Philippians 3:20) Jesus said so to Nicodemus. "Except a man be born of water and of the Spirit, he cannot enter into the kingdom of God." (John 3:5)

The Israelites of old had to re-focus their thoughts on the joys of life in the earthly Jerusalem. In a similar manner Christians today need to focus their thoughts on the heavenly Jerusalem. They need to realize anew their responsibilities as citizens of that heavenly country, before they can truly sing "the Lord's song," while yet travelling through this "strange land" on their homeward march to the New Jerusalem.

Longing for the Heavenly Jerusalem

John Newton (1725-1807), the British hymn writer, is best known as the author of the well-known hymn, "Amazing Grace." Newton has aptly portrayed the longing that every true Christian should experience, for the heavenly city, in another one of his hymns, "Glorious Things of Thee are Spoken."

During much of his early life, Newton was involved in the slave trade between West Africa and England. However, following his dramatic conversion in 1748, his life changed direction, and he began his spiritual pilgrimage. His conversion was followed shortly by his subsequent entry into the ministry. The new, heavenward direction of Newton's life was clearly evidenced by these changes. The joint publication of the *Olney Hymns* by Newton and his friend, William Cowper, bore testimony to Newton's new life in Jesus. "Glorious things of thee are spoken," which is recognized as Newton's most joyful work, appears in that collection.

The following testimonial, written by Newton himself, shortly before his death, aptly describes the unusual and colorful life of this man, one of the greatest evangelical preachers of the eighteenth century. "It is a great thing to die and, when flesh and heart fail, to have God for the strength of our heart and our portion forever."[1]

"...'Glorious things of thee are spoken" is from Part I of the Olney Hymns, and is generally considered to be

42

one of Newton's finest. It is said to be the only joyful hymn in the entire collection. ...Expressions such as "He whose word cannot be broken formed thee for his own abode," show Newton's profound respect for the covenantal promises to the Jews, as well as the local church and its ministry.[2]

The first stanza of Newton's hymn reflects the nostalgic references to the earthly Zion that are attributed to the captive Israelites, in Psalm 137:2. In the same stanza, Newton recalls several other Old Testament references to Zion as a bulwark of security (e.g., Psalm 110:2; 125:1) The second stanza alludes to Psalm 46:4, but, more specifically, points the Christian to Jesus, the Source of the water of life. In the third stanza Newton recalls God's special guidance of the children of Israel, as they marched out of Egypt, on their way to the earthly Canaan; in the same stanza, Newton reminds the Christian that God's protective power surrounds His heavenly Zion as well, along with its future citizens— "washed in the Redeemer's blood"—the only way one can be cleansed from sin, and thus find entrance into that heavenly city, the New Jerusalem. "Jesus, Whom their souls rely on, Makes them kings and priests to God. "Newton begins the final stanza of this hymn with a prayer for courage to press on toward that heavenly city, in the face of all opposition. "Let the world deride or pity, I will glory in Thy name." The hymn concludes with a bold declaration of the contrast between earthly pleasures, and the joys that await the Christian pilgrim in the heavenly city.

> "Fading is the worldling's pleasure,
> All his boasted pomp and show,
> Solid joys and lasting treasure,
> None but Zion's children know."[3]

Like the children of Israel in Babylonian captivity, Christians today find themselves dwelling in a "strange land" not unlike ancient Babylon for its corruption and idolatry, living, as we do in a society, where, all too often, the rule is "anything goes." In such a situation, the true Christian justifiably feels out of place.

The new citizenship (Philippians 3:20), which Christians receive when they accept Christ, puts a new song in their hearts. (Psalm 40:3, Psalm 96:1, Revelation 14:3) As they march onward in their pilgrimage toward the heavenly Zion, they can truly proceed "singing as we journey,"—singing the "new song' which Jesus puts in their hearts.

Every true believer needs to have that same sense of homesickness for heaven as John Newton has expressed in this beautiful hymn. Like the Israelites of old, and like John Newton, we need to pray,

> "Saviour, if of Zion's city,
> I through grace a member am,
> Let the world deride or pity,
> I will glory in Thy name."[4]

In the words of another hymn writer who echoes the same sentiments:

> "Full of joy we heavenward go,
> Singing as we journey,
> Full of joy we onward go,
>
> Singing as we journey
> Singing all our journey through,
> Singing hearts are brave and true
> Singing till our home we view,
> Singing as we journey."[5]

The Christian pilgrim, whose heart is set on the heavenly city, has no reason to hang his harps on the weeping willows, and lament, "How shall we sing the Lord's song in a strange land?" Instead, the joyful Christian can continue to have a song in his heart, "singing as we journey."

CHAPTER 6

The Song of the Angels

Joy To The World

everal centuries after the children of Israel returned from Babylon, they were once again under yet another oppressive power, the Romans. Since the time of Adam, all humanity continued to suffer under the bondage of sin. God sent a special choir of angels to make a special announcement to all mankind—the song recorded in Luke 2:8-16—good news! Once more, singing the joyful songs of Zion was possible! Although the earthly city of Jerusalem with its temple, would never again be restored to its original beauty and glory, God was seeking to focus His people's attention on the heavenly Jerusalem. The heaven-bound pilgrim, whose steps had gone astray since Adam's fall, could now make a new beginning, and resume his journey toward the heavenly Canaan.

The featured soloist in the angelic choir sang this recitative to his spellbound audience of shepherds, in the natural amphitheater of open fields outside the city of Bethlehem, while those humble shepherds listened in awe as the celestial soloist sang:

> "Fear not, for behold, I bring you good tidings of great
> joy, which shall be to all people. For unto you is born
> this day in the city of David a Saviour which is Christ

the Lord. And this shall be the sign unto you: Ye shall find the babe wrapped in swaddling clothes, lying in a manger." — Luke 2:10-12

The entire angelic choir joined in the rousing chorus, as they swelled into a grand crescendo: "Glory to God in the highest, and on earth peace, goodwill toward men. (Luke 2:14)

Whose birth were they announcing? Listen to the words penned by Emily Elizabeth Elliott, daughter of the rector of St. Mark's Church, Brighton, England. She wrote this hymn for the specific purpose of teaching children about the birth of Jesus.

> "It has a simple construction—each of the first four stanzas presents a contrast with the word *but*. Given the first two lines of each stanza, you might expect the world to welcome Christ, but no—it had no room for Him. The chorus is a natural response to the predicament, something that even a child could understand. Though the world had no room for our Lord, we have room for Him in our hearts."[6]

> "Thou didst leave Thy throne and thy kingly crown,
> When Thou camest to earth for me;
> But in Bethlehem's home was there found no room
> For Thy holy nativity."[7]

The Gospel of John describes the cold reception that Jesus received when He came to this earth. "He came to His own, and His own received Him not." John 1:11. Yes, indeed, as the second stanza of this hymn points out:

> "Heaven's arches rang when the angels sang,
> Proclaiming Thy royal degree;
> But of lowly birth didst thou come to earth,
> And in greatest humility."[8]

Responding to the Angels' Song

The remaining stanzas of this beautiful Christmas carol highlight the lack of hospitality that humankind showed to so important an infant as Jesus, the Son of God, King of the universe. However, the hymn writer echoes the open welcome with which the shepherds received Him, as they rose up immediately to go to Bethlehem and worship Him. Indeed, the words of the refrain to the first four verses represents the welcome that every true Christian should extend to this heavenly Guest:

> "O come to my heart, Lord Jesus,
> there is room in my heart for Thee."

Only as we can sincerely sing such a response to the angelic choir's anthem can we replace the lamentations of the Israelites with the joyful songs of Zion. Only then can we pick our harps off the willow trees of Babylon. Only then can we resume singing the songs of Zion. Only as we invite Jesus to occupy His rightful place as King in our hearts can we honestly make a new start on our pilgrim journey toward the heavenly Canaan. Only as we accept Him as King of Kings and Lord of Lords can we truly point our steps toward the New Jerusalem.

The children of Israel, as portrayed in Psalm 137, were justifiably tongue-tied when they voiced their reluctance to sing the joyful songs of Zion, while still living in exile, in the hostile environment of Babylon. "How shall we sing the Lord's song in a strange land?" they lamented, as they hung their harps on the willow trees. Today's heaven-bound Christian pilgrim faces a similar predicament. While earthly Babylon no longer poses a threat, all of the trials and oppressions of spiritual Babylon make this old world a place that is far from conducive to the singing of joyful songs unto the Lord. To the Christian, this world is just as much a "strange land" as was ancient Babylon to the captive Israelites. But listen! Join those humble shepherds as they keep watch over their sheep on that lonely night, about two thousand years ago. Listen with them to that angelic anthem which changed the history of the human race. Let us join them as they proceed to Bethlehem, "to see this thing which is come to pass, which the Lord hath made known to us." (Luke 2:15) For them, that joyful walk to Bethlehem was the beginning of their heavenward pilgrimage. For "whosoever will" respond in the spirit of the refrain to Emily Elliott's hymn can also be at the beginning of their heavenward journey. Make that response personal:

> "O come to my heart, Lord Jesus,
> There is room in my heart for Thee."

Have you invited Him to be the Guest of honor in your heart? If so, remember, this is only the beginning of your journey. Accepting the incarnation of Jesus is only the first step in the right direction. It is like reserving one's seat on an airplane. Merely making the reservation cannot guarantee one's arrival at his destination, unless the passenger shows up to claim his or her seat.

Hope for the Longing Pilgrim
The time is soon coming when He who "humbled Himself and became obedient unto death, even the death of the cross" (Philippians 2:8) will come back, no longer as a Babe in Bethlehem, but as "King of Kings and Lord of Lords." (Revelation 9:16) If we let him lead us throughout our pilgrim journey, then, we too can honestly join in the words of the final refrain of Elliott's hymn:

> "My hear shall rejoice, Lord Jesus,
> When Thou comest and callest for me."

On the night of Jesus' birth into this world of sin, the song of the angels was heard by those shepherds. It was not only an announcement of His birth; it was also a proclamation of the gospel; "For unto you is born this day in the city of David, a Saviour which is Christ the Lord." (Luke 2:11) Yet, for Him Who came to invite people to enter the mansions in the New Jerusalem, "there was no room in the inn" at Bethlehem. Only as we make room for Jesus in our hearts now can we be ready to welcome Him when he returns the second time.

Christian pilgrims travelling through this "strange land" ravaged by sin need no longer lament that they cannot sing the Lord's song in this "strange land." If we respond to the angelic anthem, as the shepherds did on that memorable night, two thousand years ago, and accept the heavenly citizenship which Jesus offers us now, the new life, when we can truly say, with the apostle Paul, that "Christ liveth in me" (Galatians 2:20), then we can continue to echo the angels' song as we march onward to our heavenly destination.

CHAPTER 7

The Song of the Repentant Sinner

ver since the entrance of sin, human beings have had access to God's plan of salvation. Beginning with the first promise recorded in Genesis 3:15, God has kept this world informed of His plan to redeem mankind from the captivity of Satan. Finally, "when the fullness of time was come" (Galatians 4:4), Jesus was born. The only response required of mankind was that they should acknowledge their sinful condition, and repent of their sin. In His amazing love and grace, God would accept each person who repents, and would give him or her a new heart, a new life, a new hope of eternal life.

Acknowledging our sinful condition

In the fifty-first psalm, David records his experience of repentance from his sin, and the basis on which God accepted him. David's first step was to acknowledge his transgression. "For I acknowledge my transgressions; and my sin is ever before me." (Psalm 51:3) First, David had to accept his sinful condition and his inability to help himself (Psalm 51:5; compare Romans 3:23). Next, he had to recognize that his only hope was in God, the Source of all true perfection. He had to trust that only God could cleanse him from his sin (Psalm 51:7; compare 1 John 1:9). He had to yield himself to God Who alone could create a clean heart within him (Psalm 51:10). No amount of sacrifice or other forms of work could buy salvation for David or for anyone else.

> "For Thou desirest not sacrifice; else would I give it:
> Thou delightest not in burnt offering. The sacrifices of
> God are a broken spirit; a broken and contrite heart O
> God, Thou wilt not despise." — Psalm 51:16, 17

David sensed that God had answered his prayer to "restore unto me the joy of Thy salvation: and uphold me with Thy free Spirit." (Psalm 51:12) Only then could his tongue sing of God's righteousness, and his mouth could show forth God's praises (Psalm 51:14, 15).

At times, when the Christian pilgrim recognizes that he has strayed away from the pilgrim pathway, he needs to do as David did. The words of the prophet Isaiah will then become a part of our experience as Christians.

> "And thine ears shall hear a word behind thee, saying,
> This is the way, walk ye in it, when ye turn to the right
> hand, and when ye turn to the left."— Isaiah 30:21

Accepting God's Amazing Grace

One hymn that mirrors the sentiments which David expressed in Psalm 51, is John Newton's "Amazing Grace." This hymn also expresses Newton's own experience of repentance from sin, and of the sense of God's amazing grace whereby alone he felt accepted in God's sight. In his hymn, Newton highlights the fact that he had no merits whatsoever whereby to claim God' acceptance. On the contrary, Newton recognizes that God has made His salvation available to him only through His pardoning grace as provided through Jesus.

> "Amazing Grace, how sweet the sound,
> That saved a wretch like me!
> I once was lost, but now I'm found;
> Was blind, but now I see."

In the remaining stanzas of the hymn, Newton recalls how precious that message of grace is, as he affirms, in the third stanza:

"The Lord has promised good to me,
His word my hope secures;
He will my shield and portion be,
As long as life endures."

In the fourth stanza, Newton lifts his voice in thankfulness for God's providential care over him:

"Through many dangers, toils and snares,
I have already come;
'Tis grace hath brought me safe thus far,
And grace will lead me home."

John Newton was certainly no stranger to "danger, toils, and snares." During the early part of his life, he sailed the seas, helping to transport slaves from West Africa to England. While engaged in the slave trade, he faced all the dangers that sailing vessels were subject to in his time. Neither was he unexposed to the "toils and snares" that, for some time led him far from the pathway of the Christian pilgrim.

"On March 10, 1748, during a particularly stormy voyage, while returning from Africa, when his ship was almost lost in the storm, Newton began reading Thomas á Kempis' book, *Of the Imitation of Christ.* ...Eventually, however, he felt convicted of the inhumane aspects of this work, and became a strong and effective crusader against slavery. ...At the age of thirty-nine, John Newton was ordained by the Anglican Church and began his first pastorate in the village of Olney, not far from Cambridge, England. ...Especially effective was the use of the story of his early life and conversion experience, which he told often."[9]

This was the turning point in his life. From this time forward, Newton experienced the amazing grace of God. Like David of old, Newton asked for, and received a new heart, based on God's grace, and *not* on Newton's scanty righteousness. He experienced a total transformation of his life, and acknowledged that this was only possible by the unmerited favor that God had bestowed on him through Jesus.

> "The Lord had done a marvelous thing. I was no longer an infidel. I heartily renounced my former wickedness. Conscious of God's mercy in bringing me through all my dangers, I became more serious. I was sorry for my past misspent life, and I determined to reform myself. I was freed from the habit of swearing, once a second nature to me. To all appearances, I was a new man."[10]

John Newton wraps up his poetic autobiography by bringing his experience into the context of eternal life, thus putting his entire life into the perspective of the Christian pilgrim and his ultimate goal, the heavenly Canaan:

> "When we've been there ten thousand years, Bright shining as the sun,
> We've no less days to sing God's grace, Than when we'd first begun."

When the sinner recognizes his lost condition, and allows God to help him make the necessary "U-turn" that will point him in the direction of his heavenly goal, he begins to truly experience God's amazing grace; this will put a "new song' in the heart of the repentant sinner.

David asked for, and received a new heart, and he experienced God's amazing grace. So did John Newton. So also can every repentant sinner, through the merits of Jesus alone. Acts 4:12 tells us that "there is none other name given among men whereby we can be saved." The repentant sinner who thus experiences God's amazing grace, can then continue on his heavenward pilgrimage, with a new song in his heart. Like Newton, every repentant sinner can also look forward to singing the endless praises of the One who made it possible for us to experience that amazing grace, and to keep on singing throughout eternity.

CHAPTER 8

The Song of the Obedient Believer

Caution! Pitfalls Ahead — Follow Guidelines

he Christian pilgrim who has repented of his sinful ways, and has begun his heavenward journey needs help to continue in his pathway of obedience. The pilgrim journey is not along an easy pathway. Jesus makes this very clear:

> "Enter ye in at the strait gate: for wide is the gate and broad is the way that leadeth to destruction, and many there be which go in thereat; Because strait is the gate and narrow is the way, which leadeth unto life, and few there be that find it" — Matthew 7:13, 14

Beyond Human Comprehension

William Cowper (1731-1800), was a close friend of John Newton, with whom he jointly edited the *Olney Hymns* collection referred to in a previous chapter. Cowper was a highly emotional person. His mother's death when he was only six years old made him even more emotionally sensitive[11]. Consequently, throughout his lifetime, Cowper was subject to fits of extreme melancholy. On "more than one occasion, he attempted to commit suicide by knife, by poison, by drowning, by hanging." However, despite his emotional instability, he authored several poems and hymns, many of which appear in most collections of English literature and hymns. Cowper's contributions to English hymnody continue to encourage obedient and trusting Christians everywhere. His hymns, especially the one that is highlighted in this chapter, clearly show that one can rise above the most discouraging and depressing situations in life, when one places his trust in God.

> "It seemed that hymn writing was the best therapy Cowper could get" for his mental illness. In fact, this very hymn seems to have been written as he came out of one of his periods of depression.[12]

> One story says that in his extreme depression, he hired a chaise to take him to the river Ouse to use an unfrequented spot where he planned to drown himself. By mistake, the driver took him to a popular riverside place where there were many people. Consequently, Cowper's mind changed, and, walking back home across the fields, his depression faded, and he composed these words under the title, "Light Shining Out of Darkness."[13]

The obedient believer will meet many obstacles and discouraging experiences along his pilgrimage. He will trust God at all times, even when the outlook is bleak, trusting that God Who "moved in a mysterious way" knows the end from the beginning. Even if circumstances place one among the "fearful saints," "fresh courage" is always readily available to the trusting and obedient pilgrim. "The clouds ye so much dread, Are big with mercy, and shall break with blessings on your head."

Divine Guidelines for the Christian Pilgrim
Cowper encourages his fellow-believers to place their trust in God Who "plants His footsteps in the sea, And rides upon the storm" (stanza 1). In the third stanza, he pleads with his fellow pilgrims to "Judge not the Lord by feeble sense..." and

assures them that "Behind a frowning providence, He hides a smiling face." As an obedient believer, the Christian pilgrim has every reason to join William Cowper in singing this hymn, as he sings the praises of Him Who knows the end from the beginning (Isaiah 46:10).

Choose the Narrow Way

When one chooses to walk the pilgrim pathway, and yields his life to Jesus, God's mysterious ways become manifest in his life. When the obedient Christian chooses to follow God's plan and purpose for his life, he no longer judges the Lord "by feeble sense," but will "trust Him for His grace." (stanza 3.) In faith, the Christian pilgrim looks beyond the "clouds ye so much dread" which could symbolize trials and temptations (stanza 2), beyond the "bitter-tasting" bud which could represent suffering, and even death, beyond the "blind unbelief" of those around him who would mock at his faith; he would only accept God as "His own Interpreter," knowing that, eventually, "He will make it plain." (stanza 5.)

The apostle Paul expresses this same sentiment in 1 Corinthians 13:12, where he says, "For now we see through a glass, dimly, but then, face to face."

The eleventh chapter of the Book of Hebrews features a list of individuals who personified the very obedience born of faith and trust that Cowper describes in this hymn. That list concludes with the following words, in verse 13:

> "These all died in faith, not having received the promises, but having seen them afar off, and were persuaded of them, and embraced them, and confessed that they were strangers and pilgrims on the earth."

The narrow pathway of which Jesus speaks in this text has well-defined boundaries. The psalmist David aptly summarizes these warning signs, in the very first chapter of the Book of Psalms:

"Blessed is the man that **walketh** not in the counsel of the ungodly, nor **standeth** in the way of sinners, nor **sitteth** in the seat of the scornful. But his delight is in the law of the LORD: and in His law doth he meditate day and night." Psalm 1:1, 2

No journey can ever be accomplished without walking, standing, or sitting. The original Hebrew words carry more than just the literal English meaning of these three verbs. The Hebrew word הלך halak (*haw-lak'*) which is translated "walketh" in this psalm means more than just to walk or proceed; it also carries the figurative meaning of living, or life-style. The original Hebrew word for standeth צָמַד `amad (*aw-mad'*) means to remain, to endure, to take one's stand. The third key word in the psalmist's threefold warning, "sitteth" is the translators' rendition of the Hebrew word יֹשֵׁב yashab (*yaw-shab'*) which means to remain, to abide, to dwell. This threefold warning is accompanied by a triple blessing pronounced on those who heed these precautions. This combined caution and blessing are followed by the psalmist's delight in doing God's will, because God's law is within his heart (Psalm 40:8). The writer of the New Testament book of Hebrews uses the same idea to describe the Christian's new covenant experience (Hebrews 8:10).

The obedient believer is also described in Romans 7:22 as one who "delight(s) in the law of God after the inward man." The Greek συνηδομαι sunedomai (*soon-ay'-dom-ahee*) implies more than a mere private ecstatic expression—it means rejoicing together with others — the positive antithesis of commiserating with others. This would lead a person, and his "co-rejoicers" to "sing unto the Lord a new song." (Psalm 33:3). God puts a "new song" in the mouth and heart of the obedient believer. Indeed, the author of the hymn under discussion in this chapter was one whose frequent bouts of depression and dejection were replaced by a "new song." Certainly, William Cowper's hymns, especially "God

Moves in a Mysterious Way," invite God's "fearful saints" to take "fresh courage"—thus expressing the author's invitation for others to "co-rejoice" with him.

Mysterious indeed are the ways of God. As the Christian pilgrim progresses onward in his heavenward journey, he will experience God's overruling power in countless ways. For those who willingly accept His purpose for their lives, God has prepared a city (Hebrews 11:16).

CHAPTER 9

Songs of Complete Trust in God

The Lord is My Shepherd

hristians are called upon to trust God throughout their pilgrim journey. Trusting God presents a tremendous challenge, especially as one nears the end of his earthly pilgrimage. Christians throughout the ages have taken comfort in the message of the twenty-third psalm, especially as the end of their lives draws near. These six short verses written by the shepherd-king, David, encapsulate the Christian's confidence and trust in God during this life, and on into the unknown hereafter. The first half of this beautiful hymn (for that is what a psalm is), expresses the writer's confidence in God's care and protection during this earthly life. The first verse describes the special relationship that David has with God. David's earlier experience as a shepherd, and the special relationship he would thus have had with his sheep, would certainly qualify him to picture his relationship with God in that same context.

During the seventeenth century, Scottish Christians sang some of the psalms in their worship services. The metrical psalms were also sung in their homes, during family devotions. One of the most beautiful metrical renditions of the twenty-third psalm came from the pen of Francis Rous, a member of the British parliament.

"He was dissatisfied with the accuracy of other psalm translations being used by the Puritans, some of which took liberties with the meaning to make the words rhyme. As you can see, this version is a faithful paraphrase of David's original."[14]

Of particular significance to the Christian pilgrim is the stanza in which Rous paraphrases the fourth verse of David's psalm:

"Yea though I walk through death's dark vale,
Yet will I fear no ill,
For Thou art with me, and Thy rod
And staff me comfort still."

The Christian pilgrim needs to put his total trust in the Lord, even as a helpless sheep trusts his shepherd. Especially is this important, when one walks "through the valley of the shadow of death; the Christian's trusts in God reaches beyond that valley, all the way to the eternal city. Even as Jesus, who said "I am the Good Shepherd" (John 10:11) overcame death through His own resurrection, we are to trust in Him Who also identifies Himself as "the Resurrection and the Life" (John 11:25).

The final goal of the Christian pilgrim is the heavenly homeland. While travelling this earthly pathway, the heavenly mansion should never be lost sight of. As the final stanza of Rous's paraphrase states:

"Goodness and mercy all my life,
Shall surely follow me,
And in God's house forevermore,
My dwelling place shall be."

The beautiful tune, "Crimond" with which this hymn is now associated, was composed about two centuries later. This tune was composed by Jessie Seymour Irvine, The tune derives its name from the parish of Crimond, in

Aberdeenshire, Scotland, where Jessie Irvine's father was the minister.

Trusting as the Moments Fly

The lifelong trust and confidence of the Christian pilgrim is further expressed in yet another hymn, "Simply Trusting Every Day." The author, Edgar Page Stites was a Methodist lay worker in Cape May, New Jersey. He had served in the Civil War, and later worked as a river boat pilot. It expresses the simple child-like trust in Jesus that the Christian needs to have

> "Simply trusting every day,
> Trusting in a stormy way,
> Even when my faith is small,
> Trusting Jesus, that is all."

In subsequent stanzas, the author expresses various aspects of that simple trust.

"While He leads I cannot fall," is the highlight of the second stanza. In the third stanza of this hymn, Edgar Stites expresses the need to continue singing under all circumstances during the Christian's pilgrim journey:

> "Singing if my way is clear,
> Praying if the path be drear
> If in danger, for Him call,
> Trusting Jesus, that is all."

In his final stanza, Stites reinforces the sentiment of Rous's paraphrase of the twenty-third psalm, by extending the Christian's confidence in Jesus far beyond this present life:

> "Trusting Him while life shall last,
> Trusting Him till earth be past,
> Till within the jasper wall.
> Trusting Jesus, that is all"

The refrain emphasizes the over-all theme of the entire hymn:

"Trusting as the moments fly,
Trusting as the days go by;
Trusting Him whate'er befall
Trusting Jesus, that is all."

The music for this hymn was composed by none other than Ira D. Sankey, the well-known musician who was associated with Dwight L. Moody. "This textually and musically simple expression of child-like trust in Jesus has met the daily needs of many of God's people to the present time."[15]

Both these hymns bring comfort and hope to the Christian pilgrim. Both of them provide something that the Christian can honestly sing about while on their heavenward journey. Trusting in Christ as our good shepherd we can rest, assured like the psalmist, that "I shall not want." The daily confidence and trust (...as the moments fly, ...as the days go by") expressed in the second hymn helps the Christian to develop that complete trust in Jesus for daily spiritual and material sustenance; "Trusting Jesus, that is all."

CHAPTER 10

The Song of the Remnant

The Faithful Few

esus said, "He that endureth to the end shall be saved. (Matthew 10:22) Total commitment to an unpopular cause has never been the most popular concept. If either Jesus, or any of His followers who seek to travel on this pilgrim journey were after popularity, they will never find it. Jesus also challenged those who would follow Him to choose between the broad way that leadeth to destruction, and many there be that go in thereat," and the narrow way "which leadeth unto life, and few there be that find it." (Matthew 7:13,14)

When God entrusted Gideon with the conquest of the Midianites, the would-be soldiers were given an endurance test, and, only 300 out of 32,000 passed that test. (Judges 7:2-7) Through the years of Christian history, God has been progressively testing His followers, in preparation for the final "examination"—the judgment bar of God. Through the past 2000 years, God's eternal truth has been proclaimed by a series of His messengers, all of whom were finite human beings. Their very humanity has limited each of them to a limited area of emphasis. Especially has this been so since the time of the Reformation. Martin Luther's message was based on justification by faith. Various other subsequent reformers emphasized other facets of truth. Like pieces of a jig-saw puzzle that was yet to be assembled, each facet became the center of truth for the followers of each reformer, with little or no reference to one another. But God, Who knows the end from the beginning had foretold a time when "the everlasting gospel" in its entirety was to be proclaimed to "every nation, kindred, tongue, and people." (Revelation 14:6,7) That same message also proclaimed the arrival of God's judgment hour.

William Miller, a humble Baptist layman, studying his Bible with no other scholarly helps besides his copy of *Cruden's Concordance*, began calling people's attention to the prophecies of the eight chapter of Daniel (particularly Daniel 8:14). Miller accepted the "one day = one year" understanding of Biblical time prophecies, as it applied to the 2,300 days referred to in this text. This was not a new "discovery." During the 9th century A.D., a Jewish Rabbi by the name of Nahawendi, who lived in Persia (present-day Iran) as well as other rabbis living during the intervening years, (from Spain, Portugal, Italy, France, and Algeria) taught the same.[16]

According to Miller's calculation, the cleansing of the sanctuary was to begin in 1844. However, he did not perceive the need of cleansing for the heavenly sanctuary, and, hence, he and his many followers, all of whom had expected the earthly sanctuary to be cleansed on October 22nd, 1844, were disappointed. According to them, this "cleansing" could only mean one thing—the second advent of Jesus.

Defying the Disappointment
A small group of those who had gone through that bitter disappointment began restudying the prophecies of Daniel 8 and 9 in relation to Christ's High Priestly ministry as portrayed in the Book of Hebrews. When they correlated the latter with the anti-typical Day of Atonement, the necessity to cleanse the heavenly sanctuary as a preliminary, investigative

phase of the judgment hour, as announced in Revelation 14, they realized where William Miller had been mistaken—not in his calculation of the time period which ended in 1844, but in the event which he had predicted.

Shortly afterwards, as they entered deeper into the study of God's word, they rediscovered the sacredness of God's special day of worship—the seventh-day Sabbath. The earliest of these post-Millerite Adventists were known as the "Sabbath and Sanctuary" Adventists. Eventually, in 1863, they adapted the name, "Seventh-day Adventist." They identified themselves as the "remnant" people of God, entrusted with a special message to be given to the world in these last days. The two identifying marks of that group are mentioned in Revelation 14:12—the commandments of God, and the faith of Jesus.

Espousing the plain Biblical truths that this church emphasizes has never been popular. The narrow way which Jesus spoke of would be taken only by a faithful few, even as Gideon's remnant army of three hundred were chosen by process of elimination.

In a sense, God's people are being summoned to come out of the confusion symbolized by spiritual Babylon (Revelation 18:4). Like the Israelites who felt unable to "sing the Lord's song in a strange land" (Psalm 137:4), they needed to leave Babylon's spiritual counterpart, and get back on the pilgrim pathway, heading for the New Jerusalem. Those who heed that call will be part of the "remnant" described in Revelation 12:17, as those who keep the commandments of God and have the testimony of Jesus.

Longing for Home

During the formative years of this church, the name of Annie Rebekah Smith stands out as the best known hymn writer this movement knew at the time. One of her hymns, "Long upon the Mountains, Weary" well reflects the sentiments of this poetess of the early days of Adventism. It also reflects the intensity with which the "blessed hope" of Christ's imminent return burned within those early Adventists. Even after the disappointment of 1844, recognizing that "no man knoweth the hour of Christ's return, they still expected their Lord to return soon. Annie Smith's hymn (*Seventh-day Advnetist Hymnal, no. 447*) starts off with that expression of longing:

> "Long upon the mountains weary,
> Have the scattered flock been torn
> Dark the desert paths, and dreary;
> Grievous trials have they known.
> Now the gathering call is sounding,
> Solemn in its warning voice,
> Union, faith, and love abounding,
> Bid the little flock rejoice."

Subsequent stanzas identify some of the characteristics of that little flock, including "all the ten commandments keeping," and "all the Master's precepts heeding." The third stanza emphasizes the "little flock's" hope: "Soon the pearly gates they'll enter..." The hymn closes on a note of confident longing:

> "O we long for Thine appearing,
> Come, O Saviour, quickly come."

And a prayer in the very last phrase of the final stanza:

> "Take thy ransomed children home."

In 1855, Annie Smith died of tuberculosis, at the age of twenty-seven, but not without expressing her abiding hope in the resurrection. During her short life, she had been involved in the publishing work of the church, including the editorship of the *Youth's Instructor*. Her mother, who chronicled the closing moments of Annie's life, recalled that,

"Annie exclaimed, 'Glory to God' a number of times, louder than she had spoken for a long while. 'Heaven is opened,' she said, 'I shall come forth at the first resurrection.' "[17]

Let us today reaffirm our faith in that same "blessed hope" (Titus 2:13). Rather than let it grow dim with the passing years, we need to intensify it as we continue to assemble (Gk επισυναγωγη episunagoge (*ep-ee-soon-ag-o-gay'*) = assembling—the same Greek word from which "synagogue" is derived. Today, this would involve faithfulness in church attendance. (Hebrews 10:25) The same verse also enjoins believers to assemble thus, in order to "exhort" (Gk παρακαλεω parakaleo *par-ak-al-eh'-o* = to comfort, exhort, intreat, encourage) one another. The scriptures are clear that this mutual admonishing and teaching is to continue *beyond* the time and place of regular assembly, in other words, *beyond* the limits of the church and its weekly assembly, as the apostle Paul urges his readers to "speak to one another (Ephesians 5:19), and to teach and admonish" one another (Colossians 3:16) using psalms, hymns, and spiritual songs. The text in the Book of Hebrews emphasizes that this mutual encouraging is to intensify "so much the more" as the Lord's return draws near.

Like Annie Smith, we too need to pray,

"O we long for Thine appearing,
Come, O Saviour, quickly come!
Blessed hope! Our spirits cheering,
Take Thy ransomed children home."

CHAPTER 11

The Song of
the Redeemed

Remembering the Wilderness Journey

hen the children of Israel crossed the Red Sea on their journey to the promised land, the same waters which, moments earlier, had parted for them to advance, returned to drown the pursuing Egyptian army, Moses led the Israelites in a song to celebrate this victory. It was an antiphonal anthem, which began with the words: "The LORD is my strength and song, and He is become my salvation: He is my God, and I will prepare Him an habitation; my father's God, and I will exalt him." (Exodus 15:2), with Moses' sister Miriam leading the response: "Sing ye to the LORD, for he hath triumphed gloriously; the horse and his rider hath he thrown into the sea." (Exodus 15:22)

Several centuries later, it was while the Israelites were in captivity, in Babylon, that they moaned, "How shall we sing the Lord's song in a strange land? (Psalm 137:3, 4)

Not long after that, when they finally returned to Jerusalem, and completed the rebuilding of the temple, Ezra records that the people "sang together by course" (the Hebrew word צנה `anah (aw-naw') means to sing responsively) to celebrate the occasion (Ezra 3:11).

The Heavenly Homeland Anticipated

The above high points in the experience of the children of Israel are not without their counterparts in the course of the

Christian's pilgrimage. In fact, some of these, as well as other intermediate turning points in the Christian pilgrimage have already been dealt with in the preceding chapters.

This final chapter focuses on the song of the redeemed. During the ensuing forty years, the children of Israel wandered through the "barren land" of the wilderness, and had the opportunity to learn many valuable lessons, which God sought to teach them. (The scriptures are clear that they did not always learn those lessons too well!) They did eventually arrive in the "promised land" of Canaan. Yet, despite all that they endured, their hard-earned "rest" in that land did not last forever. Eventually, Caleb and Joshua, and all the rest of them were laid to rest, awaiting the final resurrection.

The ex-captives who returned from Babylon during the time of Ezra sang to celebrate their return to Jerusalem, and the joy of worshiping in the temple which they had rebuilt. Yet, neither that temple, nor any of the singers was to last forever.

Eternal Victory Assured

The Christian pilgrim has a far stronger enemy than any Egyptian Pharaoh to overcome. But, the Christian has Jesus as the "Captain of our salvation." (Hebrews 2:10) Furthermore, the Christian, along with all those featured in the "Faith Gallery" of Hebrews 11, "having obtained a good report through faith, received not the promise: God having provided some better thing for us, that they without us should not be made perfect. (Hebrews 11:39,40.) Like Abraham, we too "desire a better country, that is, an heavenly." (Hebrews 11:16).

The book of Revelation points to the final victory celebration in heaven. All those who have overcome the beast, his image, and mark (all of which represent the false worship system) will join in singing the song of Moses and of the Lamb (Revelation 15:3,4). That victory is won "by the blood of the Lamb" (Revelation 12:11).

Lo What a Glorious Sight Appears

Seventh-day Adventist Hymnal, No. 446

As far back as 1707, Isaac Watts wrote a hymn that anticipates the glories that await the Christian pilgrim when he arrives at his destination. It reflects Watts' response to the Biblical view of the "new heavens and the new earth. (Revelation 21:1) and other scriptural descriptions of what the believer can expect to experience in the place which Jesus has prepared for those who follow Him. Watts begins with "the earth and seas are passed away," in the fist stanza. Stanza two focuses on Jesus' second advent, sitting upon His throne, "the seat of our descending King." The third stanza of Watts's hymn paraphrases the scriptural description of the heavenly experience, where Jesus" "own soft hand shall wipe the tears from every weeping eye," and where "death itself shall die." The final stanza expresses the believer's longing for that eternal place,

> "How long, dear Saviour! O how long, Shall this bright
> hour delay?"

While this hymn was written in England, by the one who is often referred to as the "father of English hymnody," it became "one of the best-loved of early Advent hymns"[18] during the 1840's in America.

Certainly in this present world, fraught with sin and all its dreadful consequences, the Christian has every excuse to experience a sense of frustration similar to that experienced by the Israelites in Babylonian captivity, when they cried out, "How shall we sing the Lord's song in a strange land?" However, the Christian pilgrim, who has made Jesus his Guide, and who has accepted the conditions of heavenly citizenship, has every reason to sing and rejoice as he continues his heavenward journey.

The Christian can express his joy in song, and praise God for providing salvation through Jesus, whose birth was announced by the angel choir. The Christian can sing and rejoice because of God's amazing grace to those who repent of their sins. The Christian can show that he "delight(s) in the law of God after the inward man" (Romans 7:22,) and express that delight in song, as he lives a life of obedience to God's will. The Christian pilgrim can also express his confidence and trust in the Lord by singing. The Christian pilgrim will also express his longing for the heavenly kingdom, in singing the "songs of Zion"—even while travelling through this "strange land."

Unwavering Loyalty

Fanny Crosby, the author of this final hymn, became blind at a very young age, as a result of a medical accident. However, her physical blindness never hindered her spiritual insight. She became one of the most prolific of American hymn writers, despite her physical handicap. She was contemplating the constant and loyal companionship of Christ with His people on their spiritual pilgrimage, when she wrote the words of this song:

> "Thou my everlasting Portion,
> More than friend or life to me
> All along my pilgrim journey,
> Saviour, let me walk with Thee."

Fanny Crosby's own account of her feelings when she wrote this hymn are as follows:

> "Towards the close of a day in the year 1874 I was
> sitting in my room thinking of the nearness of God
> through Christ as the constant companion of my pil-
> grim journey, when my heart burst out with the words:
> 'Thou my everlasting portion ...' "[19]

This hymn highlights the unfailing constancy that we can expect from Jesus, if we only commit ourselves to His guidance on our pilgrim journey. It also emphasizes the Christian pilgrim's need to remain faithful and loyal to his divine Leader throughout this pilgrim journey.

The Christian's prayer, as expressed in the second stanza, is "Not for ease or worldly pleasure," nor indeed for fame, but, "Gladly would I toil and suffer, Only let me walk with Thee."

Like Fanny Crosby, the Christian pilgrim, too, would do well to contemplate Christ's nearness while on this earthly pilgrimage, as long as life shall last.

Indeed, one would do well to pray, in the words of the final stanza:

"Lead me through the vale of shadows,
Bear me o'er life's fitful sea,
Then the gates of life eternal,
May I enter, Lord, with Thee."

The theme of this song by Fanny Crosby, as expressed in the refrain, aptly describes the Christian pilgrim's need of a constant experience of nearness to his divine Guide.

As Fanny Crosby has expressed in the refrain of this song, one needs to remain constantly close to the Lord:

"Close to Thee, Close to Thee,
Close to Thee, Close to Thee
All along my pilgrim journey,
Saviour, let me walk with Thee."

Like Fanny Crosby, we too need to maintain that unwavering loyalty, throughout our pilgrim journey, singing, "Saviour, let me walk with Thee," "all along my pilgrim journey." In times of difficulty, we will rejoice, "Gladly would I toil and suffer." Finally, "through the vale of shadows," and on to the "gates of life eternal," we can "enter, Lord, with Thee."

Let us continue "singing as we journey" through life's pilgrim journey, until; we reach that heavenly shore.

Footnotes

Part I

Introduction

[1]Ellen G. White, *Education*, (Mountian View, CA: Pacific Press Publishing Association, 1903, p.39).

[2]Lucy J. Rider, "We Are Children Of The King," *The New Advent Hymnal*, (Alma Park, England: Stanborough Press, 1952), No. 651

Chapter 1

[3]Christopher Idle, *Stories of Our Favorite Hymns*, (Grand Rapids, MI: William B. Eerdmans Publishing Company, 1980), p.51

[4]General Conference Corporation of Seventh-day Adventists, *Church Hymnal*, (Washington D.C.: Review & Herald Publishing Association, 1941), No. 409

[5]Ibid., No. 666, stanzas 4,5,6

Chapter 2

[6]William Jensen Reynolds, *A Survey of Christian Hymnody*, (New York: Rinehart and Winston Inc., 1963), p.47

[7]John A. Telford, *The Methodist Hymn-Book Illustrated*, (London: The Epworth Press, 1906), pp. 278-280.

[8]William J. Reynolds, *Songs of Glory*, (Grand Rapids, MI: Baker Books, 1990), p.63.

Chapter 3

[9]Wayne Hooper and Edward E. White, *Companion to the Seventh-day Adventist Hymnal*, (Washington D.C.: Review & Herald Publishing Association, 1988), pp. 577, 578

[10]Christopher Idle, *Stories of Our Favorite Hymns*, (Grand Rapids, MI: William B. Eerdmans Publishing Company, 1980), p.62 See also William Jensen Reynolds, *A Survey of Christian Hymnody*, (New York: Hold, Rinehart and Winston Inc., 1963), p. 37.

[11]John A. Telford, *The Methodist Hymn-Book Illustrated*, (London: The Epworth Press, 1906), pp. 348, 349.

Chapter 4

[12]Wayne Hooper and Edward E. White, *Companion to the Seventh-day Adventist Hymnal*. (Washington, DC: Review & Herald Publishing Association, 1988, pp. 427, 428.

[13]Judith P. Nembhard, "Annie Smith's Hymns of the Blessed Hope," in *Adventist Review*, August 28, 1986, pp.12-14

[14]James R. Nix, *Advent Singing*, (Washington DC: North American Division Office of Education, 1988), pp. 104, 105

[15]Edward E. White, *Singing With Understanding*, (Warburton, Victoria, Australia: Signs Publishing Company, 1968), p. 421

Conclusion of Part I

[16]Ernest K. Emurian, *Stories of Songs About Heaven*, (Grand Rapids, MI: Baker book house, 1972), pp. 60-67

[17]Ira d. Sankey, *My Life and the Story of the Gospel Hymns*, (New York: Harper & Brothers, 1906) quoted by Hooper and White, p. 466

[18]Sankey, *Sacred Songs and Solos*, Twelve Hundred Pieces, (London, England: Marshall, Morgan and Scott, 1911, Reprinted 1977), No. 958

Part II

Chapter 5

[1]John Newton, *Letters of a Slave Trader Freed by God's Grace*, (Chicago, IL: Moody Press, 1983), p.120 (Newton's Autobiography, paraphrased by Dick Bohner)

[2]Kenneth W. Osbeck, *101 More Hymn Stories*, (Grand Rapids, MI: Kregel Publications, 1985), p. 95

[3]*Seventh-day Adventist Hymnal*, (Hagerstown, MD, 1985), No. 423

[4]Ibid

[5]Lucy J. Rider, "We Are Children Of The King," *The New Advent Hymnal*, (Alma Park, England: Stanborough Press, 1952), No. 651

Chapter 6

[6]William J. Petersen and Randy Petersen, *The One Year Book of Hymns*, (compiled and edited by Robert K. Brown and Mark R. Norton) (Wheaton, IL: Tyndale house Publishers, Inc. 1996), devotional for December 8

[7]*Seventh-day Adventist Hymnal*, (Hagerstown, MD, 1985), No. 140

[8]Ibid

Chapter 7

[9]Kenneth W. Osbeck, *101 Hymn Stories*, (Grand Rapids, MI: Kregel Publications, 1982), p. 29

[10]John Newton, *Letters of a Slave Trader Freed by God's Grace*, (Chicago, IL: Moody Press, 1983), p.65 (paraphrased by Dick Bohner)

Chapter 8

[11]Edward E. White, *Singing With Understanding*, (Warburton, Victoria, Australia: Signs Publishing Company, 1968), p.462

[12]William J. Petersen and Randy Petersen, *The One Year Book of Hymns*, (compiled and edited by Robert K. Brown and Mark R. Norton) (Wheaton, IL: Tyndale house Publishers, Inc. 1996), devotional for January 22

[13]Edward E. White, *Singing With Understanding*, (Warburton, Victoria, Australia: Signs Publishing Company, 1968), p.69

Chapter 9

[14]William J. Petersen and Randy Petersen, *The One Year Book of Hymns*, (compiled and edited by Robert K. Brown and Mark R. Norton) (Wheaton, IL: Tyndale house Publishers, Inc. 1996), devotional for January 5

[15]Kenneth W. Osbeck, *101 More Hymn Stories*, (Grand Rapids, MI: Kregel Publications, 1985), p. 294

Chapter 10

[16]Francis D. Nichol, *The Midnight Cry*, (Washington DC: Review & Herald Publishing Association, 1944, pp. 132, 133), quoted by C. Mervyn Maxwell, in Magnificent disappointment, Boise, Idaho: Pacific Press Publishing Association, 1994, p. 19.

[17]Ron Graybill, "The Life and Love of Annie Smith," in *Adventist Heritage*, vol. 2. No. 1 Summer 1975, p. 21 (complete article; pp. 14-23)

Chapter 11

[18]Wayne Hooper and Edward E. White, *Companion to the Seventh-day Adventist Hymnal*, (Washington D.C.: Review & Herald Publishing Association, 1988), p. 442

[19]S. Trevena Jackson, *Fanny Crosby's Story*, (Grand Rapids, MI: Baker Book House, 1981), p. 79

Bibliography

Emurian, Ernest K. *Stories of Songs About Heaven*. Grand Rapids, MI: Baker Book House. 1972.

General Conference Corporation of Seventh-day Adventists, *Church Hymnal*, Washington, DC: Review and Herald Publishing Association, 1941.

General Conference Hymnal Committee. *Seventh-day Adventist Hymnal*. Washington, DC: Review and Herald Publishing Association, 1985.

Hooper Wayne, and Edward E. White, *Companion to the Seventh-day Adventist Hymnal*. Washington, DC: Review and Herald Publishing Association, 1988.

Hymns Ancient and Modern Revised, London, England: Hymn Ancient and Modern Ltd., 1981

Hymns for the Living Church, Carol Stream, IL: Hope Publishing Company, 1974.

Idle, Christopher, *Stories of Our Favorite Hymns* (Grand Rapids, MI: William B. Eerdmans Publishing Company 1980).

Jackson, S. Trevena, *Fanny Crosby's Story*. Grand Rapids, MI: Baker Book House, 1981.

Nembhard, Judith P. "Annie Smith's Hymns of the Blessed Hope," *Adventist Review* August 28 1986, pp. 12-14.

Nix, James R, *Advent Singing*, Washington, DC: North American Division Office of Education, 1988.

Osbeck Kenneth W. *101 More Hymn Stories*, Grand Rapids, MI: Kregel Publications, 1985,

Pilgrim Hymnal, Boston, MA:Pilgrim Press, 1931

Reynolds, William Jensen, *A Survey of Christian Hymnody*. New York: Holt, Rinehart and Winston Inc., 1963.

Rider, Lucy J. "We are Children Of The King" *The New Advent Hymnal* (Alma Park, England: Stanborough Press, 1952), No. 651.

Sankey, Ira D. *My Life and the Story of the Gospel Hymns.* New York: Harper & Brothers, 1906, quoted by Hooper and White, p. 466.

Sankey,Ira D. *Sacred Songs and Solos*, Twelve Hundred Pieces,London, England: Marshall, Morgan and Scott, 1911 (Reprinted 1977.)

Telford, John *The Methodist Hymn-Book Illustrated.* London: The Epworth Press, 1906

The Baptist Hymnal, Philadelphia, PA:American Baptist Publication Society, 1883.

The Hymnal of the Protestant Episcopal Church, New York: The Church Pension Fund, 1940.

The Methodist Hymnal, Nashville, TN: The Methodist Publishing House, 1964.

The Presbyterian Hymnal, Louisville, KY: Westminster/John Knox Press, 1990

White, Edward E., *Singing With Understanding*, Warburton, Victoria, Australia: Signs Publishing Company, 1968,)

White, Ellen G., *Education*, (Mountain View, CA: Pacific Press Publishing Association, 1903.

Appendix

For the benefit of readers who may not have access to the Seventh-day Adventist Hymnal and other Adventist hymnals referred to in the text, the author has provided this cross-reference guide (see next page) to a selection of leading hymnals containing some of the hymns mentioned.

[Note: The superscript numbers that head each column refer to footnotes at the end of the table. These footnotes refer to the respective hymnals containing the hymns listed in the table.]

Special Notes: The asterisks next to certain entries in the reference table denote the following variations in some of the hymnals:

Hymns Ancient and Modern contains John Bunyan's original version of this hymn, with the first line "Who would true valor see"

**In *Sacred Songs and Solos*, the first line of this hymn is as follows: "Oft in sorrow, oft in woe."

+ *The Presbyterian Hymnal* starts the first line of this hymn thus: "O God, in a Mysterious Way"

#In the hymnals indicated, the first line of this hymn reads thus: "Come ye that love the Lord"

Hymnal Cross-reference Guide

FIRST LINE &/OR TITLE	A&M[1]	MHB[2]	PH[3]	HPE[4]	PH[5]	BH[6]	SBH[7]	SSS[8]	HLC[9]	TLH[10]
Amazing Grace	671	92	280			492		894	288	
Come we that love the Lord (Marching to Zion)		5*				350*	165	823*	275	
Glorious Things of Thee are Spoken	522	293	446	385	267	518	152	221	209	469
God Moves in a Mysterious Way	677	215	270·	310	87	81	484	516	47	514
Guide Me O Thou Great Jehovah	296	271	281	434	93	99	520	524	448	54
He who would valiant be	293·	155		563	371		563			
O Happy Band of Pilgrims	289									
Oft in danger, Oft in woe	291			558				674··		
Simply Trusting Every Day						322		836	320	
Sometimes I hear strange music (Song of Heaven and Homeland)								958		
There's a land that is fairer than day								964		
Thou Didst Leave Thy Throne				321	326		433	35	124	
Through all the changing scenes of life	290	56			81	83	420			29
Through the night of doubt and sorrow	292			394	387		529			481
When all my labors and trials are o'er (The Glory Song)								949	538	

1. *Hymns Ancient and Modern Revised*, London, England: Hymns Ancient and Modern Ltd., 1981

2. *The Methodist Hymnal*, Nashville, TN: The Methodist Publishing House, 1964.

3. *The Presbyterian Hymnal*, Louisville, KY: Westminster/John Knox Press, 1990.

4. *The Hymnal of the Protestant Episcopal Church*, New York: The Church Pension Fund, 1940.

5. *Pilgrim Hymnal*, Boston, MA: Pilgrim Press, 1931

6. *The Baptist Hymnal*, Philadelphia, PA: American Baptist Publication Society, 1883.

7. *Service Book and Hymnal*, Minneapolis, MN: Augsburg Publishing House, 1958.

8. *Sacred Songs and Solos*, London, England: Marshall, Morgan & Scott (reprinted) 1977.

9. *Hymns for the Living Church*, Carol Stream, IL: Hope Publishing Company, 1974..

10. *The Lutheran Hymnal*, St. Louis, MO: Concordia Publishing House, 1941.

*Please see **Special Note** on page 85 for explanation of items marked by asterisks